LEADING WOMEN

COO of
Facebook and
Founder of
the Lean In
Movement

Sheryl Sandberg

AMY PETTINELLA

Cavendish
Square
New York

Published in 2015 by Cavendish Square Publishing, LLC
243 5th Avenue, Suite 136, New York, NY 10016

Library of Congress Cataloging-in-Publication Data

Pettinella, Amy.
Sheryl Sandberg : COO of Facebook and founder of the lean in movement / Amy Pettinella.
pages cm. — (Leading women)
Includes bibliographical references and index.
ISBN 978-1-62712-987-9 (hardcover) ISBN 978-1-62712-989-3 (ebook)
1. Sandberg, Sheryl. 2. Women executives—Biography. 3. Leadership in women. 4. Facebook
(Electronic resource) I. Title.

HD6054.3.P48 2014
338.7'61006754092—dc23
[B]
2014002027

Editorial Director: Dean Miller
Editor: Andrew Coddington
Copy Editor: Cynthia Roby
Art Director: Jeffrey Talbot
Designer: Amy Greenan/Joseph Macri
Photo Researcher: J8 Media
Production Manager: Jennifer Ryder-Talbot
Production Editor: David McNamara

Printed in the United States of America

CONTENTS

CHAPTER ONE

Boys Are Leaders, Girls Are Bossy

When Sheryl Sandberg got married, her younger siblings, Michelle and David, gave a toast that delighted guests with stories of Sheryl as a young girl. They joked that they were not Sheryl's younger siblings but rather her first employees. Allegedly, she taught them as toddlers to follow her around the house, listen to her monologues, and respond, "Right!"

The oldest sibling in her family and the oldest child in the neighborhood, Sheryl was known to organize clubs, which she would run, as well as plays, which she would direct. Although these stories are humorous, one thing is clear: Sheryl Sandberg exhibited extraordinary leadership skills from a very early age. More importantly, her parents did not discourage her in doing so.

Now in her forties, a billionaire, and one of the most powerful and influential women in the business world, no one can argue that Sheryl's early ambitions paid off. Still, she cringes when the word "bossy" is used to describe girls who exhibit leadership potential. She believes that derogatory words like "domineering"—which are rarely attributed to boys—discourage girls from exploring their potential.

Sheryl has recently made it her life's work to change the ways women leaders are viewed. Before women can lead, however, they must first be girls who are not afraid to lead. Sheryl knows firsthand that leading can be a scary thing for girls, and encourages them to embrace their strengths and not be afraid to show them. The world, she believes, will be a better place when women make up fifty percent of the business and political leaders and men make up fifty percent of caregivers.

A Girl Named "Girlie"

Sheryl's grandmother, Rosalind Einhorn, was born August 28, 1917, fifty-two years before Sheryl. Rosalind grew up in a poor Jewish family in tenements around New York City. Their apartment was tiny, overcrowded, and often shared with extended family members. Relatives called her male cousins by their given names, but Rosalind and her sister were called "Girlie."

During the **Great Depression**, Rosalind's parents pulled her out of high school to help support the family by performing low-paying, menial work: sewing fabric flowers onto undergarments. During those times, taking a boy out of school was unthinkable. A boy's education was viewed as the only hope for a family's future. Words such as "future" and "hope" were simply not used to describe what a girl could offer. Instead, girls were expected to help their mothers keep house and work in unrewarding and low-paying jobs to help send boys to college.

A Works Progress Administration poster advertises training for domestic servants. During the Great Depression, many girls and women were expected to leave school and take jobs performing menial labor.

A teacher, shocked that Rosalind was pulled from school, begged Rosalind's parents to reenroll her. Rosalind's parents were either ahead of their time or noted their daughter's potential. Going against the era's social grain, they put her back in school. This decision turned out to be pivotal for the family. Rosalind not only finished high school, she also attended and graduated from University of California, Berkeley, and would one day save the family business from financial ruin.

After graduating college, Rosalind returned to New York City, landing a lucrative sales position at David's Fifth Avenue. When she left David's to get married, four people were hired to replace her.

Years later, when her grandfather's paint company was on verge of failing, Rosalind took over the business. Using her knack for business, she saved her entire family—all employed by the paint company—from financial ruin. Could a woman who was forced to drop out of high school have had the wits, wherewithal, and courage to succeed in business? No one knows for sure, but most people would agree that it would be highly unlikely.

While in her forties, Rosalind was diagnosed with breast cancer, which she ultimately survived. She spent the remainder of her years raising money for the clinic that treated her by selling knock-off watches from the trunk of her car. Sheryl fondly remembers her grand-mother as the most energetic and determined person she'd ever known. Rosalind might not have known it then, but her actions would one day inspire a world-class business leader.

Parents and Siblings

Rosalind instilled in her own children the importance of education. Sheryl's mother, Adele, graduated from University of Pennsylvania in 1965 with a degree in French Literature. At that time, women typically had two career options: nursing or teaching. Adele chose to teach while working toward a **PhD** (doctorate of philosophy).

When Adele married Joel Sandberg, an ophthalmologist, or eye doctor, she dropped out of the PhD program. At the time, society viewed a man whose wife worked outside the home as weak and unable to support a family on his own. To be viewed as good wives, women were expected to drop out of the workplace.

Sheryl was born on August 28, 1969, in Washington, DC. The Sandbergs moved to North Miami Beach, Florida, when she was two. Next came a brother, David, and then a sister, Michelle, who would complete the family.

Despite raising their children in a traditional home, Joel and Adele Sandberg had high expectations for all of them. All were expected to pursue their studies diligently, engage in extracurricular activities, and perform well in athletics. Being the kid who was always picked last in gym, Sheryl began to experience insecurity at a young age. Coupled with her natural inclination to be a leader, she feared that she would not be popular among her peers. Her insecurity would follow her well into adulthood.

The Sandberg children were raised to believe that girls could do anything boys could do. Sheryl credits this early realization to a record album that her mother gave her as a little girl: *Free to Be… You and Me.* Considered revolutionary in 1972, this project of the Ms. Foundation for Women continues to be widely distributed today. The album featured prominent singers, actors, and athletes singing songs and telling stories that challenged traditional gender stereotypes.

One of the album's performers was a popular professional football player named Roosevelt "Rosey" Grier. Rosey shocked his fans with a song about why it's okay for boys to cry, something that even today boys are discouraged from doing. Sheryl was especially struck by the song "William Wants a Doll." In it, a young boy who excels in all traditional boy activities is refused his birthday wish of a doll. He ignores the taunting of his friends, brother, and sister while continuing to ask for it.

Today, Sheryl plays these songs for both her young son and daughter. She is adamant that her daughter should be free to pursue a career, raise a family, or both. She also hopes that if her son ever wishes to forgo his career to raise children, he will have the support from society that he deserves. Although known as an advocate for women's progress, Sheryl seems equally prepared to neutralize gender stereotypes altogether, which she feels harm both men and women.

Responsibility, Purpose, and Meaning

Participation in public service and activist organizations was something the Sandbergs demonstrated and expected from their children. Joel and Adele were activists for persecuted Jews in the **Soviet Union** (now the Russian Federation) in the 1970s. At the time, the Soviet Union denied its Jewish citizens the right to **immigrate** to Israel and often sent those who tried to do so to prison or labor camps.

Joel and Adele founded the South Florida Conference on Soviet Jewry to help Jews escape prison and **emigrate** from the Soviet Union. Although Joel was the president of this chapter, he is quick to point out that it was Adele who did all the work. The Sandberg home served as an unofficial headquarters for Soviet Jews wishing to escape **anti-Semitism,** as well as a transient boarding house for Jews who won the right to emigrate. On weekends, the Sandberg children often accompanied their parents to peace and freedom rallies.

By 1987, thanks in part to volunteers such as the Sandbergs and pressure from political leaders in Western countries, the Soviet Union officially permitted Jews to emigrate. As rewarding as this endeavor proved, Adele has publicly decried that her own community did not consider her contribution to the lives of Soviet Jews a

The Sandberg children often accompanied their parents to political demonstrations in support of Soviet Jews, which helped inform Sheryl's decision to serve society in some capacity.

real job. Instead, she was regarded as "just a housewife." Her unpaid work of raising children and advocating for human rights were deemed unimportant.

Despite these comments, Adele was adamant that her children grow up to serve the public in some capacity. Success to Adele Sandberg was measured not by salary but by one's contribution to society.

The Sandberg children attended public schools in North Miami Beach during the 1970s and '80s. It was a time when girls were discouraged from performing well in academics because it was not considered "cool." In spite of peer pressure to underperform, Sheryl managed to make many friends with whom she remains close today. She was elected to her class executive board, awarded an impressive internship with Congressman Lehman in Washington, DC, and graduated with a 4.64 grade point average. It came as no surprise to her friends when she was admitted to Harvard University in Cambridge, Massachusetts.

Gender Neutrality In Toys

Gender neutrality is a term used to describe the concept of raising children as individuals without regard to their gender. This concept inspires parents to encourage their children's individual strengths and interests, whether or not those strengths are traditionally accepted.

Gender bias is a preference or prejudice toward one gender over the other. Bias can be conscious or unconscious, and can manifest itself in both obvious and subtle ways. One form of gender bias is assigning gender stereotypes. For example, some argue that women are better at parenting and should raise children, while men are smarter and should pursue a challenging and demanding career. Such stereotypes often shape children's goals from an early age.

Even before they begin school, girls and boys can be shaped by the way they are taught to play. Games children play are often believed to mirror the way they view themselves in society. For example, boys are given cars and guns, and girls are given dolls. Boys play games that enable them to imagine themselves as leaders, and girls play games in which they are expected to follow orders or run a household. Opponents of these popular notions seek to discover whether these stereotypes are taught to children, or if children naturally prefer them.

In 2012, Toys"R"Us in Sweden published a gender-neutral toy catalog, which included photographs of a boy taking the temperature of a doll, a girl shooting a Nerf gun, and boys and girls playing together in a toy kitchen.

The change in the company's catalog came on the heels of a 2008 complaint made by a group of adolescents to the country's advertising representative about the "outdated gender roles" in their catalogs. Then-thirteen-year-old Hannes Psajd explained to an English-language Swedish newspaper, *The Local*, that he and his twin sister had always shared the same toys, and that he was concerned about the message being sent. "Small girls in princess stuff … and here are boys dressed as super heroes. It's obvious that you get affected by this," he told the newspaper. "When I see that only girls play with certain things then, as a guy, I don't want it." Toys"R"Us has continued its showing of gender-neutral toys in its subsequent catalogs.

CHAPTER TWO

College and Early Career

Just days after her eighteenth birthday, Sheryl arrived at Harvard, 1,500 miles (2,414 kilometers) from North Miami Beach. Filled with staggering ambition, lofty dreams, and a deep desire to make her socially conscious parents proud, Sheryl enrolled in the Harvard College of Economics.

Academic Culture Shock

Graduating at the top of her class in high school and completing an internship in Washington, DC did not prepare Sheryl for the rigors of Harvard. She received a reality check during the first day of classes. Hoping to easily satisfy a literature requirement, she enrolled in a humanities class, "The Concept of the Hero in **Hellenic** Civilization," affectionately called "Heroes for Zeroes" by her classmates. During Sheryl's first lecture, the professor asked how many of the students had read the books—without offering a clue as to the titles.

"What books?" Sheryl asked a female classmate.

"*The Iliad* and *The Odyssey*," she replied.

All of the students except Sheryl raised their hand.

Next the professor asked, "Who has read the books in the original?"

"Original what?" Sheryl asked her classmate.

"**Homeric** Greek," she responded.

At least one-third of the hands went up. For the first time in her life, Sheryl was not at the top of her class. In fact, she hovered near the bottom. Of that experience, Sheryl said, "It seemed pretty clear that I was one of the zeroes."

Not long after the reality check, Sheryl's political philosophy professor assigned a five-page paper due the following week. She was in disbelief that anyone could write a five-page paper in that short time—and keep up on all other course work. Panicked, she stayed in every night, doggedly working on the paper while her friends socialized. Despite the effort invested in the project, Sheryl received a "C" on the paper.

Sheryl notes that it was virtually impossible to get a "C" at Harvard if the assignment was submitted on time. At Harvard, a "C" grade was the equivalent of a failing grade. Humiliated about her performance and terrified for her future academic career, she sought guidance from her dorm proctor, who worked at the admissions office. After reviewing Sheryl's file, she bluntly informed her:

> *"You were not admitted to Harvard based on your academic potential. You were admitted based on your personality."*

A disappointed Sheryl picked herself up and threw herself into her studies. She was driven to work not only harder but also smarter. By the end of the semester, she learned to write five-page papers, as well as complete any other assignment that came her way. Yet despite her successes, Sheryl continually battled self-doubt, and internalizing those doubts caused her unnecessary anxiety.

Distorting the Truth

By her senior year at Harvard, Sheryl realized that internalizing self-doubt was causing her to distort the truth about her abilities, which in turn caused her insecurities to compound. Her brother, David, had since joined her at the university and enrolled in a class with Sheryl and her friend, Carrie. While Sheryl and Carrie attended all the lectures and read all the books, David chose to skip the lectures and read only one of the books.

The week before the final exam, he asked Sheryl and Carrie to give him a crash course.

After completing the exam, Carrie and Sheryl worried that they had done poorly. David, who had done little to prepare, proclaimed: "I got [an A]." Carrie and Sheryl were shocked by his arrogance—and even more surprised when they all received A grades. The experience led Sheryl to see the difference between the way women and men view their own abilities, and the debilitating effects of insecurity.

Sheryl began avoiding the temptation to assume that she would fail every task and test because a lack of self-confidence can be a self-fulfilling prophecy. "I learned over time that there was a distortion," she said. "I would never possess my brother's effortless confidence, but I could challenge the notion that I was constantly headed for failure."

Fake It 'Til You Make It

To help pay for her tuition, Sheryl taught an aerobics class on campus. Clad in a silver leotard, leg warmers, and a shiny headbands, she would try to emulate her fitness idol, Jane Fonda. Her charisma paid off. Her classes were so popular that students would line up around the building, hoping to get a spot on the gym floor. This experience taught Sheryl another valuable lesson: "Fake it 'til you make it." Performing and encouraging others to do their best required Sheryl to offer a constant smile. Sometimes the smile came easy, but on the days that it didn't, she had to fake it. In doing so, she noted that her mood was often uplifted from gloomy to cheerful.

The Girl in Right Field

Late in her undergraduate career, Sheryl took a public sector economics course with Lawrence "Larry" Summers, a professor who became instrumental in helping Sheryl establish a brilliant post-Harvard career. Initially, Sheryl failed to impress him because she never raised her hand or contributed to class discussions. Summers thought that Sheryl was at college to hang out with friends and have a good time. His suspicions

Impressing Professor Larry Summers was no small feat, but their relationship proved to be pivotal in Sheryl's successful post-Harvard career.

Crashing the System

When Sheryl attended college, the Internet was not widely available to the public. Conducting research required combing through stacks of magazines, books, and journals, or finding data on **microfiche**. In 1991, Harvard had a single computer center that few people used. Sheryl's thesis research required the tedious task of inputting data on magnetic tapes. After several hours, Sheryl overloaded the system and brought down the entire Harvard computer network. Twelve years later, another student, Mark Zuckerberg, also crashed the entire system after creating a website called "Facemash." Little did Mark or Sheryl know that together they would one day command one of the world's largest computer networking companies.

were proved wrong when Sheryl submitted the best-written midterm and final exam in the class. Impressed with her work, Summers offered to advise Sheryl on her senior thesis, which related economic inequality to spousal abuse.

As an undergraduate student, Sheryl and a friend cofounded an organization called "Women in Economics and Government." Their goal was to increase the number of women majoring in government and economics. They asked several professors to help them champion the group, but only one took up her offer: Larry Summers. Watching Sheryl lead the group and organize receptions, Larry noted her tendency to always go the extra mile. Her professionalism, dedication, and attention to detail impressed him, and he saw great potential in Sheryl.

The Impostor Syndrome

Also during her senior year, Sheryl was inducted into Phi Beta Kappa—the nation's oldest academic honor society. At the time, separate induction ceremonies were held for men and women. At the women's induction ceremony, the keynote speaker delivered a speech titled "Feeling like a Fraud," which had a profound effect on Sheryl. The speaker explained that many women feel fraudulent about their accomplishments and become uncomfortable when praised. Despite being high achievers, they feel they are somehow undeserving and worry that, at any time, someone could learn that they are frauds. The audience, made up entirely of women, all seemed to nod in agreement. Just as Sheryl suspected in high school, when she asked the yearbook committee not to name her as "Most Successful," the speaker confirmed that many women fear that success will jeopardize their likability. Sometimes referred to as "the impostor syndrome," this fear of success affects many women. Sheryl noted:

> *"The women had internalized self-doubt as a form of self-defense: people don't like women who boast about their achievements."*

The insecurity Sheryl had experienced for years started to make sense. Sheryl didn't know it at the time, but a seed was planted that would eventually help her understand what her specific contribution to the world would be.

Graduation, India, and Harvard Business School

In the spring of 1991, Sheryl had the honor of donning the Harvard cap and gown—incidentally, on that same day Barack Obama graduated from Harvard Law School. Sheryl was awarded the John H. Williams Prize as the top-graduating student in economics—an incredible feat, especially for someone who was not initially chosen for her academic potential. Her post-graduate plans included attending Harvard Law, where she hoped to get a clearer vision of her life's dream. Larry Summers, however, had different ideas for Sheryl.

Summers had recently accepted a position at the **World Bank** in Washington, DC, and hired Sheryl as a research assistant. The World Bank's mission is to reduce global poverty. The position took Sheryl to the poorest regions of India, where she supported a team working to eradicate **leprosy**. She was profoundly moved by the work the World Bank was doing, but she didn't feel it was her calling.

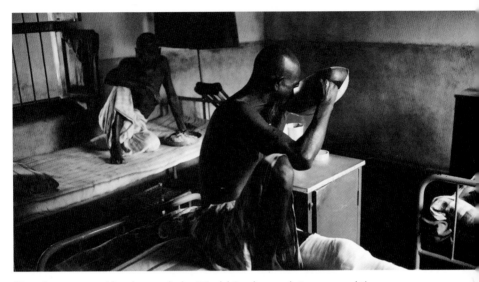

Sheryl was moved by the work the World Bank was doing around the globe, but did not feel that it was her true calling.

After completing her assignment in India, Sheryl returned to Washington, DC, with plans to attend Harvard Law School in the fall, where she had already been accepted. An economist at the World Bank, who had devoted his life to studying poverty, persuaded Sheryl to attend business school instead, where he believed Sheryl's extraordinary talents would make a bigger impact. She applied and was accepted into Harvard Business School. Once there, she joined the Nonprofit Club, which was unpopular at Harvard. During her second year of business school, she studied

Sheryl began to realize her potential while studying at Harvard Business School.

social marketing, focusing her efforts on an organ donor organization.

While studying for her Masters of Business Administration (MBA), Sheryl unexpectedly received a letter congratulating her on winning the prestigious Henry Ford Scholarship. The check was written in the amount of $714.28, which made her think that it had been split among several winners. At school the following fall, six of her male classmates made a point of telling everyone about their recent scholarship win. Unlike the six male winners, Sheryl chose to keep her award status private. "I instinctively knew that letting my academic performance become known was a bad idea." Looking back, however, Sheryl sometimes wonders if keeping this scholarship secret actually hurt her academic standing, as it has been suggested that reputation can get one as far as grades at Harvard. Reputation notwithstanding, she graduated in the top five percent of her class.

Upon graduation, Sheryl landed a job with McKinsey and Company, a prestigious business-consulting firm located in Los Angeles. Feeling challenged yet unfilled by the work, she left the firm after a year and returned to Washington, DC, determined to figure out her calling. The contacts she made while in California, however, would prove pivotal later in life.

The Treasury Department

By this time, Summers was serving as deputy secretary of the U.S. Department of the Treasury, and had hired Sheryl as his personal assistant. Soon after, Summers was

When mentor Larry Summers took the office of Secretary of the Treasury, he chose Sheryl as his chief of staff.

appointed Secretary of the Treasury by President Clinton. In turn, he appointed Sheryl his chief of staff. This made Sheryl, at age twenty-nine, Washington's youngest chief of staff. Helping oversee a $14 billion budget, Sheryl had the opportunity to participate in economic policy on both national and international levels.

Marriage

Growing up, Sheryl's parents insisted on teaching her that she could do anything a boy could do, and they provided her with invaluable tools and advice that would help her succeed. Their more subtle message, however, was that she must marry young to ensure getting "a good man before they're all taken."

With this advice in mind, Sheryl declined many promising opportunities to work overseas for fear she would not meet a man whom she or her parents would consider marriage material. While working for the Treasury, she met Brian Kraff, a local businessman. The couple married when Sheryl was twenty-four.

The marriage ended in divorce a year later, and Sheryl felt immense shame for years. Looking back, Sheryl realizes she married for the wrong reasons, and notes that she was simply not ready for what the commitment required. Although it ended amicably, she declines to publicly discuss the specifics of their divorce.

The Modern Gold Rush: Silicon Valley

When a president leaves office, all political appointees must vacate their positions. When President Clinton left office in 2001, Larry had to step down from the Treasury. Sheryl again was pounding the pavement with no idea of what she wanted to do with her life.

Meanwhile, a technology boom had taken place in California's **Silicon Valley**. Silicon Valley is a nickname for the area of Northern California near San Jose that is home to many computer and technology firms. Its name refers to semiconductors and computer chips that are made mostly of silicon and manufactured in the region.

Sheryl left Washington, DC for Silicon Valley, sight unseen. Many business people had flocked to the valley in the 1990s in hopes of launching successful Internet start-ups, dubbed "**dot-coms**." Initially the dot-coms seemed successful, which spurred investors to flood the area. This rapid rise in equity markets created the **dot-com bubble**, also referred to as the 1990's "Internet boom." By 2001, most of these start-up dot-coms were bankrupt, and many of Sheryl's government colleagues questioned her decision to stake a claim there.

Sheryl gave herself four months to land a job. Almost a year later, she was still unemployed and nearly broke. A new technology boom, however, was about to emerge, and Silicon Valley was about to explode.

CHAPTER THREE

The "It" Girl of Silicon Valley

"**M**y company would never even consider hiring someone like you."

These words came not only as a surprise but also as an insult. Two degrees from Harvard and a resume that included assistant to the chief economist at the World Bank and chief of staff for the Department of the Treasury opened no doors for Sheryl in Silicon Valley.

During one interview, Sheryl recalls an executive not only belittling her experience, but also adding that someone with a background in government could never make it in the technology sector. In hindsight, Sheryl wishes she had just walked out of the interview. Instead, she sat there biting her tongue, astonished at what was rude, unprofessional behavior. This, unfortunately, was only one example of the rude awakening she experienced during her early days in Silicon Valley. With her bank account nearly empty she knew she had to adapt—and quickly. She knew she had a lot to offer start-ups, but would she ever convince them?

Eventually, job offers began coming her way, mostly from investment banks. When it came time to decide which offer to accept, she applied her tried-and-true test to choose the best offer: creating a **spreadsheet** that compared the outlook for the companies, the position offered, and level of responsibility required for each position.

Boarding the Rocket Ship

On her list of offers was one from a fledgling unknown company with a strange name: Google. According to her spreadsheet, it was also the company with the least potential. Google was not yet three years old, had fewer than 300 employees, and had no steady revenue. Her business instincts told her to go with a known winner instead. Still, there was something about a company whose mission was to provide the world with access to information that kept her from immediately dismissing the offer.

Sheryl had become acquainted with Google's **Chief Executive Officer** (CEO), Eric Schmidt, through her work at the U.S. Treasury. For his part, Schmidt was impressed with her approach to business. After a series of interviews with Schmidt and Google's founders, she was offered the ambiguous role of business unit general manager, a newly created position. Although flattered, she found the title questionable. Google had no business units, and therefore nothing for her to manage.

The lack of concrete details about the position and direction of the company made the young entrepreneur uncomfortable. Wanting to cover all her bases, she expressed her confusion and doubts to Schmidt himself, showing him her spreadsheet of job comparisons. Schmidt read it, tossed it aside, and said,

"Don't be an idiot. This is a rocket ship. Get on it."

This was advice she could not ignore, so she jumped on the rocket ship, but not without a few doubts. She sometimes wondered if she was crazy to pass over lucrative opportunities with established companies flush with cash, but those jobs didn't make her heart pump with excitement in the same way as Google's offer.

With this experience came a valuable lesson for Sheryl. Although she appreciated certainty in her personal life, insisting on it in her professional life could cost her opportunities. She decided that in the future she would use just one criterion for considering a job offer: fast growth. She believed that companies undergoing growth spurts present extraordinary opportunities and tremendous growth to motivated employees. Conversely, a company that has a slow growth rate can create tension and politics as employees struggle to justify their positions, which can lead to career stagnation. Sheryl notes that while not everyone has an opportunity to work in a field that has start-ups, they should constantly be on the lookout for "rocket-ship" opportunities within their own companies, departments, and schools. Rocket-ship opportunities challenge employees to fix a problem or make the use of a product more practical. They require the employee or student to learn new skills or create new tools.

Sheryl laid out an eighteen-month plan for her new position at Google, which included helping her team of four employees set and reach goals for generating revenue, and forcing herself to learn new skills in a constantly changing industry. She learned quickly that, more often than not, people were happy to share their expertise if she enlisted their help.

Considering that Sheryl didn't have a long-term plan when she arrived at Google, she fared incredibly well. Eighteen months turned into six years, during which time she had been promoted to vice president of online sales and operations. Her initial team of four had grown to more than four thousand. Google had grown from a small start-up to a hundred-billion-dollar business, thanks largely in part to Sheryl's strategic decision-making abilities.

Sheryl's proudest contribution to Google, however, was establishing its philanthropic endeavors. Through its Global Impact Awards, Google has bestowed more than a billion dollars to a number of service organizations with the mission to create a better world. The programs Google sponsors include free computer science education for underprivileged students, fighting child abuse and human trafficking, protecting endangered wildlife, and empowering girls and women in third-world nations through free educational programs.

Keeping Her Private Life Private

While working at Google, Sheryl fell in love with and married long-time friend David Goldberg. Sheryl tries as much as possible to keep her family out of the public eye.

In addition to building a brilliant career, Sheryl was also building a meaningful personal life. Early in her Google career, she fell in love with her longtime friend

David Goldberg, a fellow Silicon Valley executive. When they were still friends, they went to a movie together, and she fell asleep on his shoulder, after which he realized that he was "smitten" with her. The couple wed in 2004, and has since had two children, a son and a daughter.

Despite their highly public profiles, Sheryl and David keep their family life as private, traditional, and low-key as possible. A typical Friday night in the Sandberg-Goldberg home includes eating dinner in and playing games, one of their favorites being Settlers of Catan.

Meeting Mark Zuckerberg

By 2007, Sheryl had been at Google for six and a half years, and was feeling that her professional life had become a little too certain. Wanting a new challenge, she approached Eric Schmidt once again. He offered to promote Sheryl to **Chief Financial Officer (CFO)**, but she wanted more management responsibilities. She suggested CEO, but there were already three people within the company splitting that role.

Word got out that Sheryl was looking for new opportunities, and companies began courting her. LinkedIn, the networking site geared toward professional and career development, offered her the position of CEO. *The Washington Post*, considered one of the top three newspapers in the country (along with *The Wall Street Journal* and *The New York Times*), was experiencing circulation problems and also offered Sheryl the role of

CEO. Suddenly, Sheryl had her choice of high-powered executive positions across many industries. She shocked the professional world when she chose to forgo these lucrative offers, choosing instead to work for a twenty-three-year-old named Mark Zuckerberg.

In 2007, Mark was not a household name, but the revolutionary social-networking site he created in his college dorm room (what would later be known as Face-book) had the potential to become the biggest business on the Internet. Despite his website's potential, Mark was a programmer, not a businessperson. He needed help, and

When Facebook's founder Mark Zuckerberg approached Sheryl about his new startup company, Sheryl felt the same excitement as when she first joined Google.

he needed it fast. Someone had mentioned Sheryl as a candidate, but Mark was unsure that she would leave her corner office and staff of 4,000 for a start-up such as his.

In December of that year, Mark attended a holiday party at the home of a Silicon Valley executive and spotted Sheryl as she walked through the door. Despite never having met her, he took a chance—he walked up to her and introduced himself. The two spoke for well over an hour. For the next few months, they met once a week to discuss business opportunities.

Initially, the two would meet in Mark's tiny Palo Alto apartment. Seeing that Mark had no furniture, Sheryl

Google had grown enormously under Sheryl's leadership. Leaving her corner office on the Googleplex campus for another start-up was both scary and exciting for her.

suggested that Mark join her and her husband in their home for dinner once a week. Sheryl's husband has joked that the two had a sort of courting ritual—purely professional, of course—in which they asked each other endless questions about their work philosophies and what they cherish most in their personal lives.

Mark knew that he had found the perfect candidate. Sheryl excelled at building relationships and raising revenue, neither of which Mark cared to do. He offered her the role of **Chief Operating Officer** (COO), which would make her Mark's second-in-command. Sheryl thought back to when Google offered her a similar role. She recounted the thrill of embracing the unknown, and knew she had to accept.

Sheryl did not, however, enjoy breaking the news to Google. When she told them of her plans to move to Facebook, her peers at Google tried to persuade her to stay, pointing out that her position at Google was more senior than the position Facebook was offering her. They also believed that Facebook would never give her a seat on the **board of directors**, because it had a reputation for being an "all-boys club."

A Rough Start

In March of 2008, Sheryl packed her belongings at the massive Googleplex campus and drove to her new digs at Facebook. The layout of Facebook's office stood in stark contrast to that of Google's. At Facebook, no one—not even Mark—had an office. Sheryl set up her workstation a few feet from Mark's, and he immediately delegated responsibilities to her. These included business development, international outreach, communications, public policy, and one other little thing: making Facebook profitable.

Although Sheryl was thrilled with her new job, she learned early on that Facebook employees were not excited about working for her. At thirty-eight, they considered her too old to be relevant to a new generation of web users, and they were highly suspicious that she would introduce a stiff corporate culture into their environment. She also recounts reading disparaging blog posts about her in which anonymous employees were overtly hostile, arguing that she would ruin Facebook. To make matters worse, Sheryl caught wind that Google had publicly criticized her departure and accused her of "stealing" Google employees. Being distrusted, disliked, and unwelcome was not something to which Sheryl was accustomed. Had she finally taken on more risks than she could handle?

Despite her efforts to be outgoing, open, and friendly, the staff at Facebook remained disagreeable. When a particularly nasty rumor—details of which she has declined to repeat publicly—began circulating about her, she broke down and confided in Mark. Despite her best efforts, she began to cry. Mark assured her that everyone knew that the rumor was ludicrous and encouraged her to plug away and prove people wrong. Although Mark was young enough to be her son, he proved to be a friend, and even a mentor, to Sheryl from that day forward. He helped her understand the dangers of needing to be liked by everyone, warning her that if she was pleasing everyone, then she wasn't making progress. Sheryl knew then that her best bet was to do what she had always done: to lead, and to do it bravely and boldly.

Proving Them Wrong

"Sheryl, can you come look at this? We need to see if it's something an old person can understand."

Nowadays, it's not uncommon for Sheryl to receive such requests; she doesn't take offense at them, knowing that they come from employees who truly value her opinion. Sheryl believes that effective management is nothing more than making people feel their contributions are significant to the organization. While she does foster an environment of open communication, she insists that even in heated discussions, people never raise their voices.

Mutual respect is very important to Sheryl, and she openly invites her employees to give her constructive criticism—and they do. In meetings, Sheryl dislikes the use of PowerPoint presentations because she believes that they force the presenter to unnecessarily waste time. Instead, she favors lists written in notebooks. From this, a rumor spread that Sheryl had banned the use of PowerPoint at Facebook. Finally, someone complained to her about the rule. Realizing that what she had said in passing was taken literally, she encouraged her associates to challenge her when they felt her ideas were not beneficial to the team at large. Not only did she quell the rumor, she instituted a new rule: If employees ever think that one of her ideas seems stupid, they are required to tell her so.

Although famously impatient, Sheryl's ability to gather large groups of people and come to decisions in a short amount of time is valued by many—as is her nurturing personality. Rarely does she come to a long meeting without snacks for the attendees. About this particular trait Zuckerberg says, "After Sheryl came to Facebook, I got a lot less hungry." It's not typically the job of a COO, but her colleagues have also come to rely upon her to remember birthdays, and to write perfectly worded follow-up letters to people with whom Facebook wishes to do business. These traditions have fostered a feeling of family among the Facebook team.

The New Face of Facebook

In 2012, Facebook made a dramatic decision to move the company from being privately held to publicly traded. Companies such as Facebook, which start off privately owned by an individual (in Facebook's case, Mark Zuckerberg), have the option to "go public" once they become profitable. Going public means that "shares," or stakes, in the company are sold in the stock market, and major business decisions are subsequently made by a

Sheryl's warm personality and shrewd business skills quickly made her an asset to Facebook's success.

board of directors. Such transactions are rarely smooth, and Facebook's **initial public offering (IPO)** of shares was widely considered a disaster. Shares that sold for $38 in May 2012 quickly **depreciated**. A few months later they were valued at only $10. Facebook became the punch line of every joke on Wall Street.

Facebook's headquarters in Menlo Park, California. Sheryl's leadership helped catapult Facebook into a world-class company.

Never one to accept failure, Sheryl and her staff rallied and fought their way through this rough transition period. They launched advertising on Facebook's mobile applications, which turned out to be highly profitable. By October 2013, Facebook's IPOs were valued at over

$50 a share, an increase of more than 130 percent from May of the preceding year. Facebook had become a multi-billion-dollar industry.

After selling off a few million shares of her own Facebook stock, Sheryl's personal net worth skyrocketed. Her reputation as a leader also catapulted, and once again, Sheryl was overwhelmed with offers to lead top companies. Although there's no shame in having fame and fortune, Sheryl could not stop thinking about her childhood and all the times her parents taught her that she should use her skills to help the world become a better place. Drawing on her experience in India and from her graduate school days, Sheryl helped Facebook launch a successful organ donor campaign that linked donors to organizations across the globe. Despite this, she felt as if she was overlooking something important that she could contribute, but she had no idea what her contribution could be.

CHAPTER FOUR

Success Is Not a Dirty Word

Hearing other women express discomfort with claiming power made Sheryl realize that she was not alone. She had to find a way to encourage women like herself to own their power as men do. Little by little, Sheryl's vision of what her contribution to the world should be came into focus. It started by embracing her own power—and finding the strength to share her experience with other women.

Embracing Power

Although no stranger to unsolicited job offers from major companies, Sheryl might not have realized just how far her sphere of influence had reached. In 2011, she received the honor of being named on *Forbes* magazine's annual list of most powerful women. She ranked 5th, following Pepsi CEO Indira Nooyi (4th), Brazil's president Dilma Rousseff (3rd), former U.S. Secretary of State Hillary Clinton (2nd), and German Chancellor Angela Merkel (1st).

Instead of celebrating the recognition of her contributions to the business and philanthropic worlds by a prestigious magazine, Sheryl felt embarrassed. When people congratulated her, she responded by saying that the award was silly and absurd. When colleagues shared the article on their Facebook pages, she asked them to delete the posts, telling them it made her uncomfortable. Sheryl's assistant, Camille Hart, finally pulled Sheryl aside and informed her that she was not handling success gracefully and was making herself appear insecure in front of her colleagues. Hart said,

> *"You're showing everyone how uncomfortable you are with your own power, and that's not good."*

Perhaps some people would not approve of being reprimanded by their assistant, but Sheryl was grateful for Camille's honesty—it forced her to examine her motives.

Sheryl recalled a conference she attended during her years at Google: *Fortune* magazine's "Most Powerful

Women Summit." Although it was considered an honor to be invited, Sheryl and a few other attendees joked that the name of the conference embarrassed them. Overhearing this conversation, the conference director, Pattie Sellers, an editor at *Fortune*, explained her decision to name the conference.

Fortune magazine editor-at-large Pattie Sellers (left) interviews billionaire Warren Buffet (right) about women in the workplace. Sellers, like Sandberg, is a major advocate for fulfilling professional careers for women.

Women, Sellers felt, who overcame so many obstacles to land their powerful positions, are not comfortable being called powerful. By encouraging women to describe themselves as powerful, they would eventually learn to embrace their power, and once they embraced it, they would be able to focus it. Sheryl realized that she had no problem thinking of other men and women as powerful, but could not think of herself in such terms. Internally, she knew exactly what was happening. The same voice that told her to hide her successes in business school and high school was still alive and well in her head.

Be Careful: Someone Might Notice You're a Woman

When Sheryl was invited to speak at a **TED (Technology, Entertainment, Design)** conference in 2010, she had no idea that her speech would spark what many now refer to as "the second wave of **feminism**." During this talk—which exploded on the Internet and catapulted her status as a superstar—Sheryl originally had no intention of discussing her personal struggles in rising to the top of her field. When conference organizers asked her to do just that, she responded:

> *"In the business world, you never talk about being a woman, because someone might notice you're a woman."*

Terrified that discussing the struggles of being a woman in the business world would jeopardize her career, Sheryl felt a familiar feeling: her heart beating with excitement, and an overwhelming sense of nervousness. She recognized this feeling as a telltale sign that she was on the verge of something vital. Casting aside her fears, she set out to write a speech that would help women embrace success.

Sheryl opened her TED speech with some dismal facts about the world to get the audience's attention: "Of 190 heads of state across the globe, only nine are women; of all the parliamentary seats in the world, women occupy only 13 percent of them; and in the corporate sector, women hold only 15 percent of the executive positions. Women make up 51 percent of the population, and if there are no women leaders, or if there are merely token women leaders, then women's voices will never be heard, and these numbers will never change."

Sheryl suggested that at least part of the problem with lack of leadership by women lies with women—specifically with the way women view themselves and present their success to others. She urged women to change themselves first, and the world would follow suit. "Women," she pointed out, "systematically underestimate their own abilities." All of this humility, a characteristic that women are taught to embrace since birth, Sheryl believes, causes women to not raise their hand in the classroom even when they know the answer, not negotiate for a higher salary, and not fight for promotions for which they are qualified. While women are quietly putting their noses to the grindstone and hoping to get noticed for their hard work and diligence, men are marching into meetings demanding, and getting, better opportunities. In her 2010 TED speech, Sheryl mentioned that various tests and studies have proven how this happens time and again.

For one study, Sheryl pointed out the differences between male and female college students. When asked to estimate their grade point averages, men guessed theirs slightly higher and women guessed theirs slightly lower. When asked about their accomplishments in the classroom or in business, women politely attributed their success to luck, hard work, and help from others. Men, on the other hand, proudly attributed their success to their core skills. By constantly undercutting their own abilities, women, whether they realize it or not, are announcing that they don't deserve their successes and therefore do not deserve promotions.

When Sheryl concluded her groundbreaking speech at the TED conference, she was met with a standing ovation. While some noted that she seemed nervous during the speech, others applauded her for doing something that most women would never have the guts to do: publicly encourage women to own their power, navigate their success, and give up the posture of humility that holds them back from their dreams. Her passion for the subject matter ignited a spark, which in turn would ignite a revolution.

"What Would I Do If I Weren't Afraid?"

Sheryl's TED talk video quickly went viral. With more than three million hits to date, her message is driving

Success and Likability: Heidi and Howard

Why do women keep their successes a secret while men flaunt theirs? In her TED speech, Sheryl pointed to a 2003 study conducted at Columbia University. This study revealed that success and likability are positively correlated for men and negatively correlated for women—meaning that while men will be liked for their successes, women will be disliked. The subject of this study was a woman named Heidi Roizen. Roizen began her impressive career at Apple and later went on to launch her own software firm. Being a great networker with powerful friends, Roizen later became a highly successful **venture capitalist** in Silicon Valley.

A professor at Columbia University presented Roizen's resume to his students, tasking them to determine whether they would want to hire her for their own firms. However, he made one small change to the resume: He changed her name from "Heidi" to "Howard" in half the cases. Students were then asked to read both cases and rate the subjects based on education, experience, and success.

The students agreed that both candidates had exceptional credentials, but they overwhelmingly agreed that Howard would be the better candidate of the two because he appeared to be more likeable. Heidi, they argued, came across as "selfish—not as likeable as Howard." This landmark study brought light to the discrimination that women and girls face in both the workplace and the classroom.

In her landmark speech at
Barnard College, Sheryl implored
her listeners to ask themselves,
"What would I do if I weren't afraid?"

home with a lot of women, and even some men, who believe that a more equal world is a better world. A year after delivering that powerhouse talk, Sheryl presented another pivotal speech, this time at Barnard College, a liberal arts college for women in New York City.

At Barnard, Sheryl talked openly about the ways women hold themselves back once they enter the workforce, and how the tendency to do so harms not just women, but companies, industries, and entire governments. Women make up more than half the world's population, yet their voices are not heard. This means that their needs go unmet, and their contributions to businesses and society go unnoticed.

Many sociologists agree that one of the greatest threats to mankind in the twenty-first century is the oppression of girls and women. In what Sheryl has famously referred to as an "ambition gap," she recognized a difficult but important trend among women: they are not ambitious enough. It's not their fault that much of society frowns on women in leadership roles, but it is their fault that if don't try to change society. That change, she insists, must start with women themselves. From the moment they receive their diplomas, they must fight for opportunities in their careers, and in doing so find their passion, which will keep them fighting. To find that passion, she suggests that women ask themselves one question:

"What would I do if I weren't afraid?"

To move beyond their fears, Sheryl implored the Barnard graduates to start believing in themselves "a whole lot more than they do at this moment. No one is going to promote a woman who sits on the sidelines, no matter how smart she is or how hard she has worked. Women must learn to embrace their own ambitions."

After delivering this speech, Sheryl finally understood her call to serve others: leading women to lead. She had to do more than understand her calling—she had to define it, refine it, and name it. That name would be "Lean In," which would define a not-for-profit organization and a revolutionary way of thinking. Lean In encourages women to keep going after opportunities, instead of leaning back where they wouldn't be noticed.

"You'll Never Sit On the Board"

With a newfound popularity and fan base, Sheryl began laying the groundwork to launch her organization. There was one problem, though. Despite sitting on the board of directors at Disney and Starbucks, there was still one glass ceiling she hadn't yet shattered: Facebook's board of directors.

By 2012, Facebook was considered a juggernaut of success, not just in Silicon Valley but also across every industry. Having garnered nearly a billion active users, and more than $66 billion in revenue in just over eight years of becoming incorporated, the company exceeded predictions about its potential for lasting success. At the helm of much of this success was Sheryl Sandberg.

For all its triumphs and fanfare, however, the company also had its share of bad press. From a hotly debated privacy control issue to its botched IPO launch to an unflattering Academy Award-winning film based on Mark Zuckerberg's life (*The Social Network*), Facebook was both the darling of Silicon Valley and the butt of every joke on late night television. Facebook seemed to become the company people loved to hate, even if their hatred didn't translate into boycotting the website.

One allegation in particular seemed poised to threaten the reputation of Facebook as a progressive company. Facebook, like nearly every other start-up technology company in Silicon Valley, had yet to name a female to its board of directors. With the majority of its customers being female, it seemed obvious that Facebook would profit from a female voice in its boardroom.

Sheryl was relentless in her pursuit of a seat at the Facebook board of directors table. In 2012, her hard work and determination paid off. That summer, Facebook added an eighth seat to its board and awarded it to Sheryl. Sheryl now has a voice in every major corporate decision at Facebook, which makes her message to "lean in" all the easier to deliver.

Facebook had always had something of a fraternity culture, and many people warned Sheryl that she would never sit on its board of directors.

LEAN IN
女性、仕事、
リーダーへの意欲

ェスブックのCOOが書いた
ストセラーの話題作
‧‧事と人生はこんなに楽しい

日

経

CHAPTER FIVE

Lean In

With her name appearing on various "Most" lists, including *Time* magazine's 100 Most Influential People in the World, *Fortune* magazine's Most Powerful Women in Business, and *Forbes* magazine's Most Powerful Women in the World, it seems that Sheryl would feel satisfied with her many accomplishments—that she would lean back and enjoy her success. However, leaning back is the furthest thing from her mind, and she wants it to be the furthest thing from girls and women's minds, too.

Lean In, an organization that is committed to helping women pursue their ambitions, is Sheryl's manifesto and the answer to her lifelong question of how she could change the world for the better. Launched in 2013 with the release of her book, *Lean In: Women, Work, and the Will to Lead*, it virtually became an overnight sensation and continues to be a media hot topic. The book sold more than a million copies within three months of publication, and has since been translated into twenty languages. Sheryl Sandberg became famous the world over as the leader of the second wave of feminism.

So, what does Sheryl mean by "Lean In"? When someone is telling a secret, people lean in closer to hear the information. When players huddle around a coach, they lean in to show they are listening, interested, and ready to play the game. In these ways, Sheryl wants women to lean in to their careers, to stay fully vested, and to show their boss or teacher that they are ready for the next opportunity.

Sheryl believes that many things have discouraged women from seeking and taking every advantage available, including gender discrimination in the workplace and society's discomfort in general with female leaders. Fighting these external injustices would be a noteworthy goal, but Lean In focuses on the things that women can do to improve their individual chances of being promoted to leadership roles.

Token Leaders

For the past twenty years, Sheryl has risen to the top of highly competitive fields, including government and technology. Along the way, she has seen more than a few women climb to the top only to pull up the ladder behind them, making sure that no other women could follow. It seems there is an unspoken rule in leadership: there's only room for one woman. Perhaps this stems from the negative notion that women and other minorities are merely **token leaders,** or people who are given positions of power only to make a company appear as if it embraces equality in the workplace, not because the person demonstrates superior qualifications.

Leaders who are perceived as tokens are judged more harshly than other leaders, and their successes and failures are attributed not to their actions or inactions but to their belonging to a particular **demographic** group. Being considered a token leader can cause people to view their positions as vulnerable. Because of this, leadership positions for women are perceived to be so scarce that one woman will instinctively not help another woman advance in her career for fear that she'll have to compete with her for the single leadership role.

Eliminating the negative stigma of token leadership roles for women will help balance the scales of leadership. To eliminate the stigma, Sheryl implores women to help each other along the way. As more women are rightfully promoted, the fear of being replaced by another token woman will wane, and people will begin to judge women on their merit, not on their gender.

Women, Sheryl notes, are often their own worst enemies in the workplace. Just as they underestimate their abilities in school, they do the same in their careers.

This happens because society has taught women to be humble, and men to be bold. In her book, which she describes as "a sort of feminist manifesto," Sheryl depicts how women—including herself—without realizing it, sabotage their own success. In her TED speech, she offers not only inspiration but also tools and tactics to help women get their contributions noticed. Three of those tactics were:

- Sit at the Table
- Keep Your Hand Raised
- Don't Leave Before You Leave

Sit at the Table

At extended family holiday meals, children are often asked to give up their place at a dining room table to make room for a visiting adult. Giving up a seat is considered well mannered in some situations, but not others. Sheryl has noted that too many girls grow up to give up their rightful places in business, and it starts with where they choose to sit in social, academic, and business settings.

Sheryl once hosted a meeting at the Facebook office for then-Secretary of the Treasury, Tim Geithner, and fifteen top Silicon Valley executives. As attendees entered the conference room, Sheryl showed them to the buffet and invited them to sit at the ample-sized table. The men, she noted, all grabbed their plates and sat at the table. The women, all part of Secretary Geithner's staff, sat off to the side, attempting to balance their plates in their laps.

When Sheryl invited them to sit at the table where there was plenty of room, they politely declined, keeping their seats off to the side.

Despite the fact that they were all invited to participate in the meeting, the women appeared to be spectating while the men were strategizing. The women's choice to sit on the sidelines baffled Sheryl. After the meeting, she shared her observations with the women. She implored them not only to accept invitations to sit at the table, but not to wait for an invitation in the first place. None of the men, she added, chose to sit off to the side. At first the women were slightly insulted by Sheryl's advice, but after talking to her more about it, they realized that they had missed a key opportunity to be seen as players instead of spectators.

It is possible that the women were harkening back to their childhood holiday dinners, thinking they were being polite. A woman or girl voluntarily declining her rightful seat at the table in an office or classroom, however, suggests that she is submitting to men or boys, as if they have an unspoken authority over her. Sheryl does not mean to suggest that women and girls should engage in authority and power struggles with those of the opposite sex. Rather, they should present themselves as equals, for example by sitting at the table. Doing so demonstrates that they see themselves as key players.

Sheryl has also related how not sitting at the table can directly affect a woman's salary. In her book, she cites statistics revealing that fifty-seven percent of men negotiate their salary, whereas only seven percent of women negotiate theirs. Salary negotiations take place when a person is offered a particular salary and counters with a higher salary. Many employers offer lower salaries in anticipation of the candidate negotiating for one that is higher. If a person does not negotiate, then he or she will technically be underpaid.

During an interview with *60 Minutes*, Sheryl shared that she did not initially intend to negotiate her salary at Facebook. Despite the fact that Mark Zuckerberg had recruited her for the position, she somehow felt as if she didn't deserve more than the initial offering because she wasn't sure how she would perform at the new position. In the end she did negotiate and succeeded in receiving a better financial package. According to Sheryl, there is a feeling of power one experiences by letting people know that, "You know your value."

Although the outcome was positive for both parties, Sheryl sadly realized that even after all of her leadership experience, she was still grappling with internal barriers of leveraging her own strength.

Keep Your Hand Raised

During her TED Talk, Sheryl highlighted a moment when a junior female colleague corrected her behavior, and how she handled it. A few years before launching Lean In, Sheryl held a meeting at Facebook. After the meeting, a junior female colleague approached her and said,

> *"I learned something in the meeting today. I learned to keep my hand raised."*

"During the question-and-answer period, you said you'd take two more questions. You took the two questions, so I put my hand down, and so did all the other women. Then you took more questions, all from men." Sheryl was shocked that she, someone who is committed to helping women reach their potential, didn't notice that the men kept their hands raised while the women quietly retreated.

In keeping their hands raised, the men sent a message: their questions were important and relevant to the entire group. They also sent the subtle yet powerful message that they would not be easily discouraged from reaching for new opportunities. Why did the women take their hands down? This was a question that kept Sheryl up at night. She reflected on her years of management, and realized that it was usually men who would approach her for promotions, whether they were qualified or not.

When she approached women who were qualified for higher positions, they often turned down the opportunity, explaining that they weren't yet ready, that they needed more experience, and were afraid they would fail. These women, Sheryl felt, were more than capable of performing in more demanding capacities, yet somehow, they convinced themselves that they did not deserve leadership roles. There was clearly an ambition gap among women, and helping them close it became Sheryl's life's passion. However, she first had to find out why the gap existed. What she found was that women were dropping out of the corporate race, often before they even hit their stride.

Don't Leave Before You Leave

Sheryl uses an analogy of a marathon to explain why women often drop out of the race. Imagine a career path as a marathon in which a man and a woman are both competing. At the starting line, everyone is cheering them both on with chants of praise and encouragement. As the race gets becomes more difficult, the chanting changes. To the man they yell, "Keep going! You can do it! Stay focused!" But to the woman they yell, "Be careful! It's okay to stop if you're tired! No one expects you to finish! Why are you running when you have children at home?"

Sheryl also points out how differently boys and girls are treated from birth. Girls are encouraged to follow the rules, be polite, and to support others. Boys are encouraged to ask questions, exhibit strength, and become leaders. She even notes the differences in how boys and girls are praised. Boys are praised for being clever and strong. Girls, however, are praised for being pretty and sweet, neither of which are characteristics necessary for becoming leaders.

These are the external forces that Sheryl wants women to be aware of as they begin their academic or professional careers so that they can learn to tune out the negative messages they receive. In addition to these external forces are internal forces that can prove powerful. "Don't leave before you leave," were the words Sheryl used to encourage women to stay the course in her TED talk.

Sheryl also relayed a story of a young female colleague who asked for her advice about balancing work life with family life. Sheryl asked if the colleague was expecting a child and was told that not only was the colleague not pregnant, she wasn't even married or dating. That's when it hit her—women often make provisions in their career for a family they don't even have yet.

In Sheryl's experience, a woman who worries about her ability to balance work life with family life before she even has children is often a woman who will likely never realize her full potential or satisfaction in the workplace. Opportunities for advancement will arise, and she'll make a decision based on two, five, or more years in the future—when she might have a family. Instead of taking that promotion, she'll hold herself back. Meanwhile, her male counterparts will jump at opportunities for promotion. The next thing she knows, a man who started in the company on the same day she did is now her boss. She then realizes that she is bored and that her career has not turned out to be rewarding. In this way, she left her career before she even had a child—even though she continues going to work every day.

"Don't leave before you leave," Sheryl strongly suggests to professional women. Sharing her own experience of being a working mother, she relays just how difficult it is to leave a child every day, and that if women are going to do that, then it better be for a satisfying and rewarding career. Women who choose to lean back will often return from maternity leave only to realize that their careers are neither satisfying nor rewarding—and they'll leave the workforce.

While deciding whether to be a stay-at-home mom or a professional is strictly a matter of personal choice, Sheryl implores women to continue running in the race as hard as they can until the very moment they start a family. If they get promoted and then decide to stay home, that is their choice. In the meantime, they should lean in, keep their hand raised, and pursue every opportunity. If they don't, women will continue to lag behind men in business, and their voices and decisions may never influence an organization.

Criticism

Before releasing her book, Sheryl Sandberg was a little-known name in popular culture. Although her organization, Lean In, has been applauded as a necessary change agent, she has also faced harsh and unexpected criticism. Critics assert that Sheryl blames women for not stepping up when she should be blaming companies and politicians for not fostering a more equal world. Others say that her advice is only good for women who are already millionaires and can afford nannies for their children. Still others believe that she encourages the breakdown of the family unit

To some, the ideas in *Lean In* seem controversial. Sheryl is often forced to justify her thoughts during interviews.

by encouraging women to focus on their careers at the expense of their children.

Her proponents, however, argue that these criticisms tell only half the story. For example, Sheryl makes it clear in her book that she chooses to focus on how women can improve their chances of being promoted, not how businesses make it difficult for women to be promoted. The tools she offers for success—sit at the table, keeping your hand raised, don't leave before you leave—are things that any woman can do regardless of how much money she has. Finally, Sheryl does not tell women to choose a career over children, but rather to pursue their career as diligently and intelligently as possible before they have children.

Lean In: How Does It Work?

Lean In, the organization, is the hands-on extension of Sheryl's book. It's a highly organized grass roots organization that encourages women (and men) to advance their careers by offering members three important tools for success: community, education, and "circles." Joining Lean In is free and can be done at leanin.org.

This online community encourages the exchange of ideas and information about career development. It also hosts blogs where users can write about their own success stories. The only rule for online postings is that they must be about success, not disappointments, as this keeps members feeling motivated instead of discouraged. Lean In also offers opportunities for continuing education. Its library boasts a collection of free online lectures presented by various industry leaders and experts on a plethora of topics that include negotiating, power and knowledge, and leadership. Finally, Lean In offers a resource called "circles," which are small groups of women and men who meet monthly to discuss their goals and obstacles, and to offer each other support and feedback. The website offers all the resources someone needs to start a circle in their own community.

Although it was initially geared for working-age women, a few circles for teenagers have begun to spring up. These circles, sometimes led by a teacher or coach at school, help girls embrace success in both school and extra-curricular activities. It also helps counter the ambition gap in high school, college, and beyond. Members of these teen circles are reporting a high degree of satisfaction from their circle of peers. With *Lean In* the book and Lean In the organization, Sheryl has created a framework of support and resources that are reaching hundreds of thousands of people around the world.

CHAPTER SIX

We've Come a Long Way, but...

B y the time Sheryl delivered her 2010 TED talk "Why There Are Too Few Women Leaders," she had had a lifetime of success to draw on. However, a seat on Facebook's board of directors eluded her. Never one to give up, she knew that she and other women still had a long way to go. With that in mind, her speech began with these words:

> "We're lucky. We don't live in the world that our mothers and grandmothers lived in where career choices for women were so limited. We live in a world where we have basic civil rights, yet amazingly we still live in a world where some women don't have them."

Through the Lean In movement, Sheryl wants women to acknowledge and appreciate the progress that women's rights activists have made in the past. She also wants women of today to pick up the torch to honor those women by continuing to achieve equality, particularly by becoming leaders in business, not-for-profit agencies, and government.

Today in the United States, women can become successful on any career path they choose. The problem is that most women are not becoming experts is certain fields. There are many explanations, for example, as to why many women are not pursuing careers as engineers, astronauts, inventors, or public officials. None of those explanations include, "They're not smart enough," or "They're not working hard enough." As a result, they are missing opportunities to climb the ranks and become leaders in these arenas. Sheryl chooses to focus on one reason for the stagnation: Women and girls are not keeping their hands raised. Finding out why is the first step toward correcting it.

Women are "Taking Over"

In 2013, a record twenty women held seats in the U.S. Senate, representing 20 percent of that elected legislative body. On the heels of that unprecedented election, some media outlets proclaimed, "Women are taking over the Senate." Three things were troubling about these sentiments. First, 20 percent is a minority. For every four men who make laws that affect every citizen of the country, there is only one woman doing the same. Second, it's impossible to "take over" the Senate, because seats are elected. Third, men have never been accused of "taking over" the government, even though they have always held the vast majority of seats. Most troubling of all, the tone seemed to stoke a certain fear: women who have power are dangerous.

Such negative messages can be distressing to all members of society, especially to girls and women. If it is reinforced that they are not welcome in leadership roles, and that they will be persecuted in some way for wanting to enter such an arena, then they won't want to become leaders, even if they would excel in the position.

Is Feminism a Dirty Word?

Feminism is an ideology held by many women and men who maintain that women should have rights and opportunities equal to those of men. Feminism is not the belief that women should hate men or have special advantages over them. Many opponents of feminism seek not only to dismiss the need for equality among men and women, but also to scorn and shame anyone who believes in equality. The campaign against equality has been so effective that "feminism" has become a dirty word.

Sheryl struggled with the word "feminism" for most of her life, even though she has always been gravely offended by sexist attitudes and has spent years striving for equality for all women. Even while at Harvard—where she founded the campus group that encouraged women to enter government and economics—she did not self-identify as a feminist. Many women who believe in equality are afraid to identify as feminists. Doing so, they fear, will associate them with the negative stereotypes that characterize feminists as man-haters.

Many women and girls fear being labeled as feminists because they feel men and boys will not like or respect them. Even in classes on feminism held on today's college campuses, female students are quick to point out that even though they want equal rights, they don't want to be labeled as feminists.

Gratitude, humility, grace, and service—these are all characteristics that girls and women are taught to revere. To a reasonable degree and in varying circumstances, these are excellent qualities, but boys should be equally encouraged to express them. Instead, they are taught that it is their birthright to sit at the table and make all the decisions while girls are taught to sit off to the side. This type of behavior not only ensures their continued advantage in an unfair system, it breeds fewer opportunities for equal success among girls and women.

Malala Yousafzai is a sixteen-year-old Pakistani girl who knows firsthand just how far some people will go to ensure that women do not have equal opportunities. When she was a child, the **Taliban** came to her village, systematically bombed schools for girls, and imposed

Despite having an attempt made on her life, Malala Yousafzai remains fearless in her advocacy for the education of girls around the world.

laws that made it illegal for women and girls to even leave their homes. Many who did not obey these laws were executed in the streets. When Malala was fourteen, she began blogging about her experiences, and soon after, the Taliban issued a death threat against her. Later that year, while riding a bus home from school, she was shot in the head. Narrowly surviving, she went on to speak publicly about the oppression of women and girls in her country. In 2013, she became the youngest person ever to be nominated for the Nobel Peace Prize.

Girls in the United States and many other countries do not have to worry that they will be assassinated for wanting an education. They know that when they turn eighteen they will have the right to vote. If they choose to attend college, they can pursue any major area of study they wish. However, achieving goals beyond these basic rights remains difficult task for many girls.

Many people believe—and encourage girls and boys to believe—that for a girl to want anything more than basic rights is unreasonable, ungrateful, and worse, "unladylike." Some people will even go so far to say that a girl who has a natural ability or desire to lead is sinful and should be discouraged from doing so. Assigning negative and hostile labels to such girls is the first step in keeping them from even pursuing their goals.

One way Sheryl hopes that Lean In will help circumvent these negative stereotypes is by encouraging people to pay close attention to the words they use when describing women and girls. "Bossy," is a divisive and derogatory word that is rarely, if ever, attributed to boys. By calling a girl who has natural leadership abilities "bossy," a message is sent that in order to be liked, girls should follow orders, not offer solutions.

The first step in correcting an injustice is speaking up against it—yet girls are continually taught that silence and politeness are the highest virtues to which they can aspire. Girls who do speak their minds are often **marginalized** or ridiculed. Boys who speak their minds are praised as being brave leaders. Sheryl, with these words, encourages people to think twice about the words they choose to describe girls:

> *"That little girl's not bossy. That little girl has executive leadership skills."*

77 Cents

When it comes to demanding equality, what does this "silence" cost girls and women? A lot. One of the most obvious things it costs them is money—twenty-three cents an hour, to be exact. Although the reasons for it vary and are hotly debated, the U.S. Census Bureau found in 2012 that for every dollar a man makes, a woman earns only seventy-seven cents.

"What's the big deal about twenty-three cents an hour?" many people argue. For one thing, it translates to a loss of about $1,600 per year. Over the course of a forty-five-year career, the difference is $72,000.

For minorities, this wage gap is even worse. African American women earn only sixty-nine cents for every dollar an African American man is paid. Hispanic women earn just fifty-eight cents for every dollar a Hispanic man earns. So why is there such a stark disparity in wages?

A major contributor is that a larger majority of women work lower-paying jobs. Feminists—both men and women—are scrambling to find out why women are either relegated to, or are settling for, these jobs. Other studies show that even when men and women have the same occupation and level of education, the wage gap remains. Despite the Equal Pay Act of 1963, many businesses have managed to find loopholes that enable them to pay women less money than they pay men for the same work. Currently, many senators and members of Congress are fighting to close these loopholes, but many believe that day is a long way off.

Financial security is a major step toward independence, and independence is a precursor to power. Unfortunately, many people are still threatened by women who embrace independence because they believe that women either do not deserve power or will somehow abuse it. Sheryl urges girls and women to ask themselves if they believe that they deserve the same rights and opportunities granted to men, and if they do, to proudly bear the label of "feminist."

In her book, Sheryl relayed a story that her mentor Larry Summers shared with her. In the 1940s, Larry's mother was a brilliant, sought-after economist, something unprecedented for women of that era. When Standard Oil hired her in 1947, her boss was ecstatic to have her on staff, exclaiming, "I am so glad to have you. I figured I'm getting the same brains for half the amount of money." It somehow escaped the boss how this "compliment" was an insult. At that time, women felt they had no choice and that they were lucky to even be given a job.

Since her TED talk, Sheryl has seen progress in both the way that women present themselves in business and educational settings, and in how society views women who embrace ambition. Sheryl jokes that CEOs complain to her, "You're costing me so much money!" in response to women successfully negotiating for better salaries. Her response: "I'm not sorry at all!"

"Woman" is Not an Adjective

Feminist leader Gloria Steinem once said, "Whoever has power takes over the noun—and the norm—while the less powerful get an adjective." This one of Sheryl's favorite quotes because it speaks so clearly to the issue of women's contributions being taken less seriously than those of men. When "woman" is used as adjective, people tend to forget the noun it modifies—lawyer, doctor, CEO, president—and focus only on the gender. If a man holds a powerful title, such as president or prime minister, his title is not modified by the word "man" or "male" because it's assumed that a powerful leader is male. The modifier "female" is used because it suggests that it is unexpected or unusual for a woman to be a leader.

It is Sheryl's wish that someday "woman" will no longer be used as an adjective or modifier. She dreams of day when people will not be threatened by successful women leaders or by girls who wish to become leaders. After all, she says, "No one wants her achievements modified." Lastly, Sheryl wants women to help each other achieve this goal instead of pulling up the ladder behind themselves once they reach the top rung of leadership.

By leaning in, sitting at the table, and keeping their hands raised, girls will grow up to be women who are respected for their opinions, revered for their strength, and above all, trusted to be leaders of schools, companies, and nations.

Sheryl is a highly sought-after speaker, and uses her influence to encourage women and girls to keep their hands raised and to lean in to challenging opportunities.

Timeline

1991

Graduates from Harvard; joins Larry Summers at the World Bank

2004

Marries David Goldberg

2006

Named to *Fortune* magazine's list of Most Powerful Women in the World; remains on the list for the next seven years

1969

August 28: Sheryl Sandberg is born in Washington, DC

1996

Joins Larry Summers at the Department of the Treasury, becoming Washington's youngest chief of staff

Graduates from North Miami Beach Senior High School

1987

Leaves for Silicon Valley; joins Google

2001

Gives birth to her son

2005

Graduates from Harvard Business School with an MBA

1995

2008

Joins Facebook as chief operating officer

2010

Delivers her groundbreaking TED speech "Why There Are Too Few Women Leaders" and gains rock-star status in the business world

2012

Oversees Facebook's first initial public offering (IPO); named to Facebook's board of directors; named on *Time* magazine's 100 Most Influential People

2014

At the age of 44, Sandberg becomes one of the youngest billionaires in history

Gives birth to her daughter; meets Mark Zuckerberg

2007

Delivers life-changing commencement speech at Barnard College

2011

Named board member of The Walt Disney Company

2009

Writes best-selling book, *Lean In: Women, Work, and the Power to Lead*; launches LeanIn.org

2013

SOURCE NOTES

Chapter 1

P. 15, Landes, David, "Toys'R'Us Scolded for Gender Discrimination," www.thelocal.se/20091006/22504.

Chapter 2

P. 18, Sandberg, Sheryl, *Lean In: Women, Work, and the Will to Lead* (New York, NY: Knopf, 2013), p. 31.

P. 18, Sandberg, Sheryl, *Lean In: Women, Work, and the Will to Lead*, p.31.

P. 19, Sandberg, Sheryl, *Lean In: Women, Work, and the Will to Lead*, p.31.

P. 20, Sandberg, *Lean In: Women, Work, and the Will to Lead*, p. 33.

P. 20, Sandberg, *Lean In: Women, Work, and the Will to Lead*, p. 33.

P. 20, Sandberg, *Lean In: Women, Work, and the Will to Lead*, p. 33.

P. 21, Hempel, Jessi, "Sheryl Sandberg: Facebook's new number two to Zuckerberg," http://money.cnn.com/2008/04/11/technology/facebook_sandberg.fortune/index.htm.

P. 24, Auletta, Ken, "A Woman's Place," www.newyorker. com/reporting/2011/07/11/110711fa_fact_auletta.

P. 26, Sandberg, *Lean In: Women, Work, and the Will to Lead*, p. 42.

P. 28, Sandberg, *Lean In: Women, Work, and the Will to Lead*, p. 17–18.

P. 28, Sandberg, *Lean In: Women, Work, and the Will to Lead*, p. 17–18.

P. 28, Sandberg, *Lean In: Women, Work, and the Will to Lead*, p. 17–18.

Chapter 3

P. 31, Sandberg, *Lean In: Women, Work, and the Will to Lead*. p. 57.

P. 31, Sandberg, *Lean In: Women, Work, and the Will to Lead*. p. 57.

P. 33, Auletta, "A Woman's Place."

P. 33, Sandberg, *Lean In: Women, Work, and the Will to Lead*, p. 58.

P. 33, Sandberg, *Lean In: Women, Work, and the Will to Lead*, p. 58.

P. 34, Sandberg, *Lean In: Women, Work, and the Will to Lead*, p. 58.

P. 34, Sandberg, Lean In: Women, Work, and the Will to Lead, p. 59.

P. 36, Kent, Muhtar, "TIME 100: The List, Sheryl Sandberg, Chief Operating Officer," content.time.com/time/specials/packages/article/0,28804,2111975_2111976_2112093,00.html.

P. 39, Auletta, "A Woman's Place."

P. 39, Auletta, "A Woman's Place."

P. 40, Auletta, "A Woman's Place."

P. 40, Auletta, "A Woman's Place."

P. 40, Auletta, "A Woman's Place."

P. 40, Sandberg, *Lean In: Women, Work, and the Will to Lead*, p. 88.

P. 40, Sandberg, *Lean In: Women, Work, and the Will to Lead*, p. 88.

P. 41, Sandberg, *Lean In: Women, Work, and the Will to Lead*, p. 51.

P. 41, Gara, Tom, "Exclusive: First Look At Sheryl Sandberg's New Book," blogs.wsj.com/corporate-intelligence/2013/02/05/sheryl-sandbergs-fight.

P. 42, Kent, "TIME 100: The List, Sheryl Sandberg, Chief Operating Officer."

Chapter 4

P. 48, Sandberg. *Lean In: Women, Work, and the Will to Lead*, p. 43.

P. 49, Howard, Caroline, "Forbes Announces World's 100 Most Powerful Women 2011," huffingtonpost.com/forbes-most-powerful-women_n_934312.html.

P. 50, Sandberg, *Lean In: Women, Work, and the Will to Lead*, p. 51.

P. 50, Sandberg, *Lean In: Women, Work, and the Will to Lead*, p. 51.

P. 50, Walters, Helen, "Ban the Word Bossy," blog.ted.com/2013/12/05/sheryl_sandberg_tedwomen2013.

P. 51, "Sheryl Sandberg: Why We Have Too Few Women Leaders," www.ted.com/talks/sheryl_sandberg_why_we_have_too_few_women_leaders.html.

P. 51, "Sheryl Sandberg: Why We Have Too Few Women Leaders."

P. 51, "Sheryl Sandberg: Why We Have Too Few Women Leaders."

P. 52, "Sheryl Sandberg: Why We Have Too Few Women Leaders."

P. 52, "Sheryl Sandberg: Why We Have Too Few Women Leaders."

P. 53, Routson, Joyce, "Networking is More Than Lots of Names, Says Heidi Roizen," www.gsb.stanford.edu/news/headlines/heidiroizen.html.

P. 57, "Transcript and Video of Speech by Sheryl Sandberg, Chief Operating Officer, Facebook, 2011," barnard.edu/headlines/transcript-and-video-speech-sheryl-sandberg-chief-operating-officer-facebook.

P. 57, "Transcript and Video of Speech by Sheryl Sandberg, Chief Operating Officer, Facebook, 2011."

Chapter 5

P. 62, Sandberg, *Lean In: Women, Work, and the Will to Lead*, p. 51.

P. 64, Sandberg, *Lean In: Women, Work, and the Will to Lead*, p. 51.

P. 64, Sandberg, *Lean In: Women, Work, and the Will to Lead*, p. 28.

P. 65, Sandberg, *Lean In: Women, Work, and the Will to Lead*, p. 28.

P. 65, Sandberg, *Lean In: Women, Work, and the Will to Lead*, p. 28.

P. 65, Sandberg, *Lean In: Women, Work, and the Will to Lead*, p. 28.

P. 66, Sandberg, "Sheryl Sandberg Pushes Women to 'Lean In.'"

P. 66, Sandberg, "Sheryl Sandberg Pushes Women to 'Lean In.'"

P. 67, Sandberg, "Sheryl Sandberg Pushes Women to 'Lean In.'"

P. 67, Sandberg, *Lean In: Women, Work, and the Will to Lead*, p. 62.

P. 68, Sandberg, *Lean In: Women, Work, and the Will to Lead*, p. 100.

P. 69, Swisher, Kara, "Sheryl Sandberg Will Become COO of Facebook," kara.allthingsd.com/20080304/sheryl-sandberg-will-become-coo-of-facebook/?-mod=ATD_search.

P. 69, Sandberg, "Why We Have Too Few Women Leaders."

P. 69, Sandberg, "Why We Have Too Few Women Leaders."

P. 70, Sandberg, "Why We Have Too Few Women Leaders."

P. 70, Sandberg, "Why We Have Too Few Women Leaders."

P. 71, Kolhatkar, Sheelah,"What Sheryl Sandberg Doesn't Get about the Gender Gap," businessweek. com/articles/2013-09-25/what-sheryl-sandberg-doesnt-get-about-the-gender-gap.

P. 71, Kolhatkar, "What Sheryl Sandberg Doesn't Get about the Gender Gap."

P. 71, Holmes, Anna, "Maybe You Should Read the Book: The Sheryl Sandberg Backlash," newyorker. com/online/blogs/books/2013/03/maybe-you-should-read-the-book-the-sheryl-sandberg-backlash. html

P. 72, Sandberg. "Why We Have Too Few Women Leaders."

Chapter 6

P. 75, Sandberg, "Why We Have Too Few Women Leaders."

P. 76, Sandberg, *Lean In: Women, Work, and the Will to Lead*, p. 28.Roberts, Cokie and Steve Roberts, "The Women Are Taking Over," dailyherald.com/article/20131018/discuss/710189961.

P. 78, Sandberg, *Lean In: Women, Work, and the Will to Lead*, p. 28.Williams, Elizabeth, "Why Are Women Scared to Call Themselves Feminists?" salon. com/2012/12/03/why_are_women_scared_to_call_themselves_feminists.

P. 81, Sandberg, *Lean In: Women, Work, and the Will to Lead*, p. 28.Montini, Laura, "Let's Ban the Word Bossy," inc.com/laura-montini/sheryl-sandberg-lets-ban-the-word-bossy.html.

P. 82, Sandberg, *Lean In: Women, Work, and the Will to Lead*, p. 28.Sandberg, *Lean In: Women, Work, and the Will to Lead*, p. 158.

P. 83, Sandberg, *Lean In: Women, Work, and the Will to Lead*, p. 28.Sandberg, *Lean In: Women, Work, and the Will to Lead*, p. 4.

P. 83, Walters, Helen, "Ban the Word Bossy."

P. 83, Sandberg, *Lean In: Women, Work, and the Will to Lead*, p. 140.

P. 84, Sandberg, *Lean In: Women, Work, and the Will to Lead*, p. 140.

GLOSSARY

anti-Semitism Discrimination against, or prejudice or hostility toward, Jews as a religious, ethnic, or racial group.

board of directors An elected or appointed group of individuals who oversee a company or organization and make decisions on major company issues.

Chief Executive Officer (CEO) The highest-ranking executive manager of a company or organization; responsibilities include developing and implementing high-level strategies, making major corporate decisions, and managing the overall operations and resources of a company.

Chief Financial Officer (CFO) The senior manager responsible for overseeing the entire company's financial activities; duties include financial planning and monitoring cash flow.

Chief Operating Officer (COO) The senior manager who is responsible for managing the company's day-to-day operations; reports to the CEO.

demographic A section of the population sharing common characteristics, such as gender, race, religion, age, or socio-economic class.

depreciate To diminish in value over time.

dot-com A company that sells products and/or services on the Internet.

dot-com bubble The rapid rise in equity markets fueled by investments in Internet-based companies; also referred to as the 1990's "Internet boom."

emigrate To leave a country where one was born or raised in order to settle permanently in another country.

feminism The belief that men and women should have equal rights and opportunities.

gender bias Prejudice or discrimination based on a person's gender.

gender neutrality Terms or expressions suitable for, applicable to, or common to both male and female genders.

Great Depression (1929–1939) An economic recession that followed the October 1929 stock market crash; it caused massive levels of poverty, hunger, unemployment and political unrest lasting nearly a decade.

Hellenic The branch of the Indo-European language family comprising classical and modern Greek.

Homeric Relating to the style of Homer, an ancient Greek epic poet.

Iliad, The Greek epic poem (attributed to Homer) describing the siege of the ancient Greek city of Troy.

immigrate To enter, and usually become established in, a country of which one is not a native.

Initial Public Offering (IPO) The first sale of stock by a private company to the public.

leprosy A serious and contagious disease that causes painful rough areas on the skin and that badly damages nerves and flesh.

marginalize To put or hold a person (or group of people) in a powerless or unimportant position within a society or group.

microfiche A sheet of film that has very small photographs of the pages of a newspaper, magazine, etc.

Odyssey, The A sequel to *The Iliad* in which the Greek hero Odysseus journeys home after the Trojan War.

PhD Doctorate of Philosophy; the highest college degree that is typically obtained after three years of graduate study and completion of a dissertation.

Silicon Valley A region in Northern California near San Francisco noted for its concentration of high-technology industries.

Soviet Union Formerly a communist country in Eastern Europe and northern Asia; established in 1922, it dissolved in 1991.

spreadsheet A computer generated grid document that organizes data into columns and rows.

Taliban A fundamentalist Islamic militia in Afghanistan.

TED (Technology, Entertainment, Design) A nonprofit organization devoted to "Ideas Worth Spreading."

token leader A derogatory term describing a person who is given a leadership title, often based on a minority status, but no responsibilities or authority.

venture capitalist An investor who provides money to startup companies or supports small companies that wish to expand but do not have access to public funding.

World Bank An international financial institution that provides loans to developing countries for capital programs.

FURTHER INFORMATION

Books

Sandberg, Sheryl. *Lean In: Women, Work, and the Will to Lead*. New York, NY: Knopf, 2013.

Johnston, Andrea. *Girls Speak Out*. Berkley, CA: Celestial Arts, 2005.

Articles

Anne-Marie Slaughter, "Yes, You Can: Sheryl Sandberg's 'Lean In,'" *The New York Times*, March 2013.

Jodi Kantor, "A Titan's How-To on Breaking the Glass Ceiling," *The New York Times*, February 2013.

Ken Auletta, "A Woman's Place: Can Sheryl Sandberg upend Silicon Valley's male-dominated culture?" *The New Yorker*, July 2011.

Kurt Eichenwald, "Facebook Leans In," *Vanity Fair*, May 2013.

Susan Adams, "10 Things Sheryl Sandberg Gets Exactly Right In 'Lean In,'" *Forbes*, March 2013.

Websites

Lean In

www.leanin.org

The official website for Sheryl Sandberg's movement, this site offers an array of resources, including news and articles, lectures by business leaders, a community dedicated to discussion of women's and business issues, and more.

Sheryl Sandberg's Twitter Page

twitter.com/sherylsandberg

See what Sheryl Sandberg is up to. Her Twitter account is updated frequently with photos, articles, and news.

Makers

www.makers.com/sheryl-sandberg

Watch a video of Sheryl giving advice on a variety of topics, including being a geek, a successful business leader, a women's advocate, and a working mom.

TED

www.ted.com/speakers/sheryl_sandberg

On Sheryl's page on TED.com, you can watch recordings of her speeches about the state of women in business and the future of women leaders, explore blog posts, and read a brief biography.

BIBLIOGRAPHY

Ashton, James. "Sheryl Sandberg: Facebook's Billion-Dollar Brain." *The Independent*, May 19, 2012.

Auletta, Ken. "A Woman's Place." *The New Yorker*, July 11, 2011.

Bassett, Laura. "Women Still Earned 77 Cents On Men's Dollar In 2012: Report." *Huffington Post*, September 17, 2013. Accessed November 28, 2013. www.huffingtonpost.com/2013/09/17/gender-wage-gap_n_3941180.html.

Bort, Julie. "Sheryl Sandberg: This is the Most Gratifying Thing I've Ever Done." *Business Insider*, November 20, 2013. Accessed November 28, 2013.

Eldon, Eric. "Sheryl Sandberg, Facebook's Long-Time COO, Becomes First Woman On Its Board Of Directors." *Tech Crunch*, June 25, 2012. Accessed November 29, 2013. techcrunch.com/2012/06/25/facebooks-board-of-directors-adds-its-first-woman-sheryl-sandberg-its-long-time-coo.

Gara, Tom. "Exclusive: First Look At Sheryl Sandberg's New Book." *Wall Street Journal*, February 5, 2012.

Goodman, Ellen. "Brilliant Boys, Good Girls': Sexism In The Classroom." *The Boston Globe*, February 28, 1994.

Helft, Miguel. "Sheryl Sandberg: The real story." *Fortune*, October 10, 2013. Accessed November 24, 2013. money.cnn.com/2013/10/10/leadership/sheryl-sandberg-mpw.pr.fortune/index.html.

Hempel, Jessi. "Sheryl Sandberg: Facebook's new number two to Zuckerberg." CNN Money, April 11, 2008. Accessed November 25, 2013. money.cnn.com/2008/04/11/technology/facebook_sandberg.fortune/index.htm.

Holmes, Anna. "Maybe You Should Read the Book: The Sheryl Sandberg Backlash." *The New Yorker*, March 4, 2013

Howard, Caroline. "Forbes Announces World's 100 Most Powerful Women 2011." *Huffington Post*, August 24, 2011. Accessed: December 3, 2013. www.huffingtonpost.com/forbes-most-powerful-women_n_934312.html.

Howard, Caroline. "The World's Most Powerful Leaders 2013." *Forbes*, May 22, 2013.

Husain, Mishal. "Malala: The Girl Who Was Shot for Going to School." *BBC News Magazine*, October 7, 2013. Accessed December 1, 2013. www.bbc.co.uk/news/magazine-24379018.

Kent, Muhtar. "TIME 100: The List, Sheryl Sandberg, Chief Operating Officer." *Time*, April 18, 2012.

Kolhatkar, Sheelah. "What Sheryl Sandberg Doesn't Get about the Gender Gap." *Business Week*, September 25, 2013.

Landes, David. "Toys'R'Us Scolded for Gender Discrimination." *The Local: Sweden's News in English*, October 6, 2009. Accessed December 1, 2013. www.thelocal.se/20091006/22504.

Luscombe, Belinda. "Confidence Woman." *Time*, March 7, 2013.

Nathan, Sara. "From Teenage Aerobics Instructor to Facebook's Billion-Dollar Woman and Is the Next Stop the White House? The Astonishing Rise and Rise of Sheryl Sandberg." *The Daily Mail*, March 1, 2013.

Newsweek Staff. "Sheryl Sandberg, An Inside View of Facebook." *Newsweek*, October 4, 2008.

Rankin, Jennifer. "Sheryl Sandberg sells $90m of Facebook stock." *The Guardian*, August 12, 2013.

Raice, Shayndi, and Lublin, Joann S. "Sheryl Sandberg Joins Facebook Board." *Wall Street Journal*, June 25, 2012.

Sandberg, Sheryl. *Lean In: Women, Work, and the Will to Lead.* New York, NY: Knopf, 2013.

"Sheryl Sandberg: Why We Have Too Few Women Leaders." Filmed December 2010. TED video, 14:55. Posted December 2010. www.ted.com/talks/sheryl_sandberg_why_we_have_too_few_women_leaders.html.

"Sheryl Sandberg Pushes Women to 'Lean In.'" Filmed March 2013. 60 Minutes video, 11:40. Posted March 2013. www.cbsnews.com/news/sheryl-sandberg-pushes-women-to-lean-in-11-03-2013.

Swisher, Kara. "Sheryl Sandberg Will Become COO of Facebook." NPR: All Things Digital, March 4, 2008. Accessed November 27, 2013. kara.allthingsd.com/20080304/sheryl-sandberg-will-become-coo-of-facebook/?mod=ATD_search.

Transcript and Video of Speech by Sheryl Sandberg, Chief Operating Officer, Facebook, 2011. Video, 19:45. barnard.edu/headlines/transcript-and-video-speech-sheryl-sandberg-chief-operating-officer-facebook.

Transcript and Video. www.cbsnews.com/news/sheryl-
   sandberg-pushes-women-to-lean-in-11-03-2013.

Walters, Helen. "Ban the word bossy. Sheryl Sandberg
   lights up TED Women 2013." TED Blog, December 5, 2013. Accessed November 25, 2012.
   http://blog.ted.com/2013/12/05/sheryl_sandberg_
   tedwomen2013.

INDEX

ABOUT THE AUTHOR

Amy Pettinella is an author and playwright who lives in Indianapolis, Indiana. She has worked in the information technology sector since graduating from college, and has watched nearly every female mentor she's ever had bump her head on the glass ceiling. In writing about the life and philosophy of Sheryl Sandberg, she encourages readers to overcome what Sandberg refers to as "the ambition gap." Pettinella has also authored *Queen Latifah: Award-Winning Actress and Hip-hop Activist* in Cavendish Square's Leading Women series.